World Religions

Christianity

Katherine Prior

W
FRANKLIN WATTS
LONDON·SYDNEY

This edition 2005

Franklin Watts
96 Leonard Street, London
EC2A 4XD

Franklin Watts Australia
Level 17/207 Kent Street
Sydney, NSW 2000

© Franklin Watts 1999

Editor: Sarah Snashall
Art director: Robert Walster
Designer: Simon Borrough
Picture research: Sue Mennell

Religious consultants:
Angela Wood, teacher, broadcaster and
curriculum adviser in religious education
Lesley Prior, Advisory teacher and
lecturer in religious education

A CIP catalogue record for this book is
available from the British Library.

ISBN 0 7496 6419 3

Dewey classification 200

Printed in China

Picture credits:

Cover: Impact Photos (Christophe Bluntzer)
(right); Rex Features (Patsy Lynch) (inset)

Andes Press Agency/Carlos Reyes-Manzo pp. 18,
23b, 26t, 28b, 29t; Axiom Photographic Agency pp.
13 (James Morris), 16b (James Morris); Bridgeman
Art Library pp. 5b (Galeria degli Uffizi, Florence), 9
(The Morning after the Resurrection, Burne-
Jones/Christies Images), 10 (The Matyrdom of St.
Cosmas and St. Damien, Fra Angelico/Louvre,
Paris, 12 (Martin Luther, Lucas Cranach/National
Museum of Stockholm), 14 (Kungl. Biblio Teket,
Stockholm), 20 (Baptism of Christ,
Veronese/Church of the Redentore, Venice), 22
(The Adoration of the Magi, Burne-
Jones/Hermitage, Leningrad); CIRCA Photo
Library/ICOREC p. 25c; Eye Ubiquitous pp. 11r
(David Cummings), 25l (Lawrence Fordyce), 29b
(Dave Fobister); Hutchison Library pp. 4 (Michael
Macintyre), 15t (Maurice Harvey), 17b (Melanie
Friend), 24 (Andrey Zvoznikov); Image
Select/CFCL p. 23t; Impact Photos pp. 5t (Caroline
Penn), 11l (Julian Calder), 19t (Mohamed Ansar)
21t (Caroline Penn), 25t (Steve Parry), 26b
(Christophe Bluntzer), 27 (Rachel Morton); (c)
National Gallery, London (The Annunciation, Fra
Filippo Lippi/NG666); Panos Pictures pp. 6 (Bruce
Paton), 16t and b (James Morris), 19b (Betty Press);
Rex Features pp. 7r (P. Massey), 17t (Patsy Lynch),
21b McNamee), 28t; (c) Tate Gallery, London 1998
(Jesus Washing Peter's Feet Ford Madox
Brown/N01394) p. 7l; Franklin Watts p. 15b

maps pp.8, 13 Julian Baker

CONTENTS

✝ ONE GOD

CHRISTIANS BELIEVE IN ONE GOD. God created and loves the world and everything in it. God lives in heaven, but heaven is not a physical place. Christians cannot describe what heaven or God look like.

Holy Trinity

Christians believe that God exists as three beings – God the Father, God the Son and God the Holy Spirit. This is called the Holy Trinity, and all three beings are equally important.

The Christian scriptures say that God loved the world but saw that people committed sins (wrongdoings) against his law. God sent his only son, Jesus Christ, to earth to show people how to live good lives. Jesus was persecuted (ill-treated) on earth and died a horrible death, but Christians believe that, when he died, he took the punishment for all the sins of the world.

A young Christian prays to God.

Forgiven for sins

The Christian faith is based on a belief that if Christians ask God for forgiveness for their sins, they will be saved after death and live for ever with God in heaven. They will not have to be punished for their sins, because Jesus had suffered for them.

These Christians are worshipping God by singing his praises.

Holy Spirit

Christians believe that the Holy Spirit is God's presence on earth. They believe that the Holy Spirit helps them to keep their belief in Jesus Christ.

This painting, by an unknown artist, shows how Jesus was killed by being nailed to a cross.

God so loved the world that he gave his only Son, so that everyone who believes in him may not perish but may have eternal life.

John 3. 16

BEING A CHRISTIAN

ANYONE CAN BE A CHRISTIAN. They do not have to be born into Christianity. Anyone who believes in Jesus Christ and follows his teachings is a Christian.

Having faith

To become a Christian a person must put their whole faith in God and trust that he will look after them and guide their souls to heaven. The person must believe that Jesus died as a punishment for their sins.

For Christians, faith is the strength to believe that God is real and is caring for them, even though they cannot see him or have obvious proof that he exists.

Loving the lowly

Jesus had many followers when he was on earth. They were not the rich and respectable people of the Jewish society in which Jesus lived, but poor fishermen and serving women. They were unpopular tax collectors and outcasts like prostitutes and spies. Christians believe that they should follow Jesus's example and love everyone – the poor, the sick, unpopular people and even criminals.

This nun has dedicated her life to Jesus Christ and to helping poor people.

How to be a Christian

Christians see Jesus's life on earth as a perfect example of how to behave. Jesus's message was one of love and peace.

Jesus taught that people should not worry about building up wealth on earth. Instead they should build up spiritual treasures in heaven. This means that they should spend time praying to God and living according to God's law.

Christians should be charitable, like this woman who is helping to deliver soup to homeless people.

Jesus taught his followers to be humble. This painting by Ford Madox Brown shows him washing the feet of his disciple Peter.

Christians believe that God loves everyone. They therefore believe that they should be kind and loving to people around them, even if the people around them are their enemies. Christians should never argue or be violent, and should be loving and forgiving to people who are violent to them.

Jesus warned his disciples, the men who followed him, that they would be persecuted. He told them that they should not strike back, but remain peaceful and be glad that they were able to show God how much they loved him. God would reward them in heaven for their actions.

THE LIFE OF JESUS

JESUS WAS BORN IN THE LAND OF ISRAEL about 2000 years ago. He was born to Mary and Joseph, Jews from Nazareth in Galilee. Before her marriage to Joseph, Mary had been told that, although she was a virgin, she would have a child who was the son of God.

The angel Gabriel visits Mary to tell her she will have God's son, by Fra Filippo Lippi.

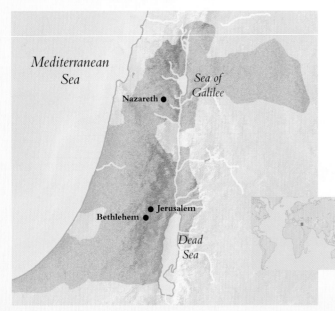

This map shows the area of Israel where Jesus spent his life.

Jesus's birth

The Bible says that before Jesus was born, Mary and Joseph went to Bethlehem to register for the census. The inns were all full so they took shelter in a stable. There Mary gave birth to Jesus.

An angel appeared to nearby shepherds and told them that their saviour had been born. The shepherds rushed to see. From the east came three wise men. They had followed a bright star which shone above the stable. They came to worship the baby they called the King of the Jews.

Jesus's life and teaching

In his youth, Jesus studied the Jewish scriptures. In his early thirties he began preaching in public. He performed miracles and cured the sick. He called upon his fellow Jews to repent their sins. Jesus had many followers and, from these, he selected twelve men as his disciples. At this time, the Jews were ruled by the Romans and they hoped for the arrival of the Messiah, a saviour to free them from Rome and restore their kingdom. Jesus's followers believed he was the Messiah.

The Jewish leaders believed that Jesus's teaching broke God's law. The Roman governor found him guilty of trouble-making and sentenced him to death by crucifixion.

> He is despised and rejected of men; a man of sorrows and acquainted with grief.
>
> 2 Isaiah 53. 3

This painting by Edward Burne-Jones shows Jesus standing by the empty tomb.

Death and resurrection

Jesus was crucified – nailed to a cross and left to die. At three o'clock the sky went dark, and Jesus died. His disciples took his dead body off the cross and placed it in a tomb. But on the third day, when his women followers went to the tomb, they found it empty – Jesus had risen from the dead. This is called the resurrection. Jesus spent forty days with his disciples before God took him up into heaven.

✝ EARLY CHRISTIANS

SOME OF JESUS'S DISCIPLES became his apostles, or messengers, and began to tell the world that God had sent his son to earth to save people from their sins. Belief in Christ soon spread across the Roman Empire, but the Romans persecuted the early Christians.

First churches

Jesus had told his followers to spread the good news of his coming to earth, and one of the first men to do this was the apostle Paul. He had originally persecuted the Christians, but after he had a vision of Christ, he travelled all over Cyprus, Turkey and Greece, converting people to Christianity.

The early Christians had to worship in secret. They gathered together in small congregations (groups), each with a local leader, or bishop. As Christianity spread, however, the persecution lessened and in 313CE the Emperor Constantine promised the Christians that they could worship safely in public.

Many early Christians, like St Cosmas and St Damien shown here, were killed for their beliefs. The painting is by Fra Angelico.

East and west

The two most important bishops in early Christianity were the patriarchs of Rome in the west and Constantinople (modern Istanbul) in the east. Eastern Christians always worshipped in Greek, the language of the apostles. Since about 200CE, however, the western Christians had begun to pray and worship in Latin, the language of the Romans.

Two churches

The two groups grew further apart until, by about the 11th century, Christianity had split into two completely separate branches: Catholicism in the west, ruled over by the Pope in Rome, and Orthodox Christianity in the east, ruled over by the Patriarch of Constantinople. There is still a Pope and a Patriarch today.

This priest is Patriarch of the Orthodox Church in Russia.

The Pope is the leader of all the Roman Catholics in the world.

We believe in one God, the Father, the almighty, maker of heaven and earth, of all that is, seen and unseen.

The Nicene Creed

One creed

Today there are many kinds of churches. Every Sunday, however, millions of Christians are united when they repeat the same creed, or statement of belief.

SPREADING THE WORD

IN THE 16TH CENTURY, western Christianity was divided further. Some Christians in northern Europe believed that the Catholic church had drifted away from the original Christian message and that some of their rituals were wrong. They wanted to follow the true Christian message. They were called 'Protestants'. This movement was called the Reformation.

Martin Luther

The Reformation started when Martin Luther (1483-1546), a German monk, began to criticize the Catholic church. He did not believe that good works or charity alone could get a person to heaven, as some priests taught. Luther believed that salvation was a divine gift given by God in return for absolute faith in Jesus Christ. After Luther's work in Germany, Protestantism spread across northern Europe.

Today many Christians are Protestants and there are many kinds of Protestant church: the Anglican Church and the Baptist Church are the largest.

Martin Luther, painted by Lucas Cranach.

Evangelists and missionaries

Even as Christianity was dividing again, it was spreading throughout the world. Many early Christians, like the apostle Paul, were called evangelists, from the Greek word *euangelos* which means 'bringing good news'.

Many Christians since Paul have continued to be evangelists. In the 18th century there was an evangelical revival in Britain among Protestants who wanted to bring the knowledge of Christ to the poor who were often ignored by the Anglican Church. The evangelists also worked as missionaries in Africa, Asia and the Pacific islands and among the African slaves in the USA and the Caribbean. Today, there are many missionaries from Africa who travel around the world telling people about Jesus Christ.

There is a strong evangelical tradition today, especially in the USA, where preachers often use television, popular songs and high-tech roadshows to persuade non-believers to turn to faith in Christ.

This map shows the areas of the world where Christianity is the main religion.

Jesus said '...go and proclaim the Kingdom of God.'

Luke 9. 60

A Roman Catholic nun teaches schoolchildren in Nigeria about Jesus Christ.

THE BIBLE

THE BIBLE is the sacred book of Christians. It contains histories, songs and letters written by different authors, all of whom Christians believe were inspired by God. There are two main sections: the Old and the New Testaments. A testament is a promise.

Old and new

After Jesus's resurrection, his followers continued to read and obey the Jewish holy books as before. They saw these Jewish holy books as the word of God and they loved them because they predicted the coming of Christ. For Christians, these Jewish books became the Old Testament.

The first Christians did not write down Jesus's life, but simply talked about it to anybody who would listen. About 150 years after Jesus's birth, scholars began to create the New Testament by collecting accounts of Jesus's life and teaching. It begins with the accounts, called the Gospels, by Jesus's followers Matthew, Mark, Luke and John. Gradually, other writings were added to the New Testament, including letters of advice written by the apostle Paul to the early Christians.

Early copies of the Bible were often beautifully decorated like this one.

What language for the Bible?

Originally the Old Testament was written in Hebrew and the New Testament in Greek, but as Christianity spread across the Roman Empire the Bible was translated into Latin. In 1533 Martin Luther translated the Bible into German. The first official Bible in English was published in 1611.

In the beginning
was the Word,
and the Word
was with God,
and the Word
was God.

John 1. 1

Many Christian families read the Bible together as an act of worship and prayer at home.

The most common book in the world

Today the Bible is published in hundreds of different languages. Every day, millions of Christians read it for advice and comfort and for proof of God's love for them. They discuss the Bible's meaning together in Bible-classes. Passages are read aloud in church services.

Passages from the Old and New Testaments of the Bible are always read during church services.

WORSHIPPING GOD

CHRISTIANS COME TOGETHER to worship God in a building called a church. Some churches are huge buildings, beautifully lit with stained-glass windows and topped with tall spires, but a church does not have to be grand. A simple hall where a congregation meets regularly is as much a church as a grand cathedral.

The cross in this church reminds the congregation of Jesus's suffering.

A special day

Christians keep Sundays, the day on which Jesus rose from the dead, as their holy day of the week. They go to church to give thanks to God.

In regular church services there are readings from the Bible and often the priest or minister preaches a sermon showing how the Bible can guide people in their lives today. The congregation prays and sings hymns together and each person makes a small donation of money to be used for charitable work. In some churches and ceremonies, flowers, candles and incense add to the atmosphere.

All churches have a table called an altar where the Eucharist is prepared (see page 21).

Priests and Ministers

Every church has a leader called a priest, or, often in Protestant churches, a minister. These leaders have been especially trained by their church to carry out the sacred rites of Christianity. Ordinary Christians often seek the advice of their priest when they are unsure what God wants them to do, they feel they have committed a sin, or they need reassurance of God's love for them.

These women are bishops – senior priests of the Anglican Church.

Sing hymns and psalms to the Lord with praise in your hearts.

Ephesians 5. 19

In some churches, Christians sing and dance to show their love for God.

Music

Many Christians praise God by singing hymns. Psalms (songs from the Bible) and hymns were sung or chanted in the earliest churches, often by a choir of monks, and modern services still have many sung parts.

Black-led churches in America have many popular hymns. Their gospel songs grew out of early slave churches in which the slaves sang of the suffering people on earth longing for heaven and of the coming of God's glory. This tradition lives on in the joyous singing and dancing which fill Afro-Caribbean churches around the world today.

17

✝ PRAYER

PRAYING IS TALKING DIRECTLY TO GOD. It is an act of faith. When a Christian prays no booming voice answers. Instead, the person praying feels what God is saying to them.

Private or public

Some Christians kneel down to pray; others simply lower their heads. This shows that they are respectful and humble but it also helps them to concentrate.

Prayers can be said anywhere. They can be private or they can be said out loud, sometimes with a whole congregation in a church. A prayer can be a fixed set of words or a person can simply say what they feel in their hearts. During prayer, Christians praise God and ask God for help in being a Christian.

Prayers begin with a greeting such as 'Our Father', and end it with the word 'Amen', which means 'truly' or 'so be it'.

This woman is using a string of beads, called a rosary, as she prays.

The Lord's Prayer

One of the most important prayers is the Lord's Prayer, which Jesus himself taught to his disciples. It is a short prayer, simple and direct; it offers praise to God and asks for his assistance and protection from evil. It is said by congregations in most church services.

Our Father in Heaven,
hallowed be your name.

Opening of the Lord's Prayer

The Rosary

Christians in the Roman Catholic Church often say a series of prayers, recited in a particular order, called the Rosary. The repetition of the prayers helps the person praying to concentrate purely on God. To help them remember their place, Roman Catholics may use a string of prayer beads, also called a rosary. As they say each prayer they pass a bead through their fingers.

Roman Catholics often pray to Mary, mother of Jesus, and it is her prayer, the Ave Maria or Hail Mary, which features most in the Rosary.

Prayer time is a time not only for praising God but also for thought and reflection.

During prayer, Christians often press their hands together in front of them as a sign of respect to God.

THE SACRAMENTS

A SACRAMENT is a public act performed by Christians which shows that they have received God's grace – his divine assistance and blessing. Most Christians recognize two sacraments: baptism and Eucharist (also called the Lord's Supper, Mass or Holy Communion).

Baptism

Baptism is a ceremony in which new Christians are sprinkled with water, or immersed fully in water, to symbolize the washing away of their sins and to announce their entry into the Christian church. Adults who want to be baptized must ask God to forgive their sins and must promise to obey God's teachings. Jesus Christ himself was baptized by John the Baptist in the River Jordan. After his resurrection, he commanded his disciples to baptize new believers in the name of the Father, Son and Holy Spirit.

The first people to be baptized were adults, but now it is common to baptize babies. Babies cannot make promises themselves, so their parents or godparents promise that they will bring them up as good Christians.

The 16th-century Italian artist Paolo Caliari Veronese imagines what it looked like when John the Baptist baptized Jesus Christ.

Eucharist

The night before he was crucified, Jesus had a meal, called the Last Supper, with his disciples. During it, he took a piece of bread, gave thanks to God, broke it, and said to his disciples, 'This is my body, which is given for you. Do this in memory of me.' He then did the same with a cup of wine, saying 'This cup is God's new covenant (promise), sealed with my blood. Whenever you drink it, do so in memory of me.'

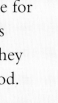

As she drinks from the cup of holy wine, this woman gives thanks for Jesus Christ having died to save her.

In services called Eucharist, priests and ministers repeat Christ's actions and words at the Last Supper with consecrated (sacred) bread and wine.

A minister blesses the bread during the sacrament of the Eucharist.

'This is my body, which is given for you. Do this in remembrance of me.'
Luke 22. 19

After Christians have had the Eucharist, they are thankful for the great sacrifice Christ made for them. They feel that their sins have been forgiven and that they have renewed their love of God.

21

† CHRISTMAS

EVERY YEAR CHRISTIANS celebrate several festivals. They celebrate Jesus's life at Christmas and Easter and the coming of the Holy Spirit at Pentecost. Some Christians have festivals for the Virgin Mary and the saints. Christmas celebrates the birth of Jesus.

This tapestry, designed by Edward Burne-Jones, shows the wise men visiting Jesus.

'I am bringing you good news of great joy for all the people: to you is born this day in the city of David a Saviour, who is the Messiah, the Lord.'

The angel of the Lord to the shepherds

Luke 2. 10–11

Advent

For Roman Catholics and Protestants, the season of Advent, or the time of coming, begins four Sundays before Christmas. There are special church services during Advent in which Christians hear again the story of Jesus's birth as told in the Bible.

Christians also spend Advent preparing for Christmas Day. In schools, children often act out the story of Jesus's birth, and, in town squares, churches, and at home, Christians put up nativity scenes and decorated Christmas trees.

At Christmas, children often act out the story of Jesus's birth.

Orthodox Christians begin Advent in November. They observe the season with fasting. To fast is to stop eating or to eat very little over a number of days. It is a way of trying to control the body and to concentrate on God.

Christmas Day

On Christmas Eve and Christmas Day itself, Christians attend church services, where often they sing carols – hymns which tell the Christmas story. Afterwards they eat a festive meal together and exchange presents. Giving presents is an important part of Christmas. It reminds Christians that God made the gift of his son to them.

These carol-singers are raising money to give to poor and hungry people all over the world.

✝ EASTER

EASTER IS THE MOST IMPORTANT FESTIVAL in the Christian calendar. In the days before Easter, Christians remember Jesus's terrible death on the cross. Then, on Easter Sunday, Christians celebrate his resurrection from the dead.

Then Jesus said, 'Father, forgive them; for they do not know what they are doing.'

Luke 23. 34

Lent

Before Easter there is a forty-day period of fasting called Lent. It is a time when Christians concentrate on prayer and religious study. Many Orthodox Christians still observe strict fasts, and do not eat meat, eggs or milk during Lent and only take one simple meal in the evening. Other Christians may not fast as strictly as this, but may give up luxury foods.

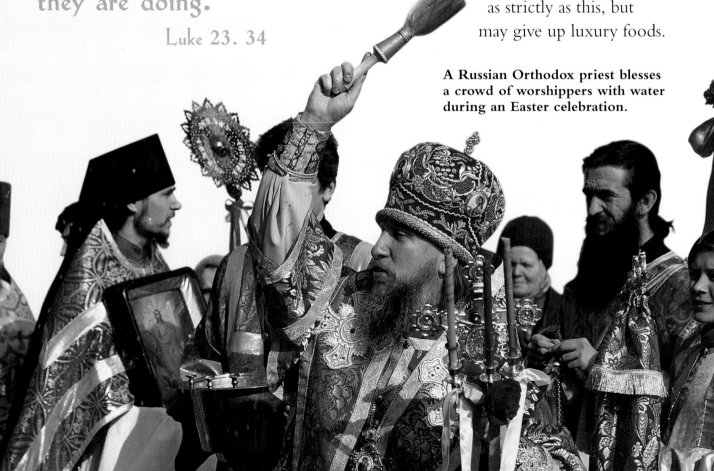

A Russian Orthodox priest blesses a crowd of worshippers with water during an Easter celebration.

Holy Week

The week before Easter is called Holy Week. It begins with Palm Sunday which commemorates Jesus's entry into Jerusalem in the last week of his life when he was greeted by cheering crowds waving palm leaves. On the Thursday of Holy Week, Maundy Thursday, Christians remember Jesus's last meal with his disciples, the Last Supper.

The Friday of Holy Week is Good Friday (the name probably comes from God's Friday). On Good Friday, Christians remember Jesus's crucifixion and painful death. This is a solemn day of prayer.

A plaited palm-leaf is held behind the priest at a church service on Palm Sunday in Spain.

A Christian in the Philippines acts out Jesus carrying his cross to the hill where he will be crucified.

Easter

On Easter Sunday Christians celebrate Jesus's resurrection from the dead. For Christians it is a sign that there is life after death, and they give thanks that, because of Jesus's sacrifice, they too can hope for eternal life in heaven after they die. Often they exchange gifts of painted or chocolate eggs as a symbol of new life.

Roman Catholics have a special candle called a paschal candle which is lit and carried into the dark church where members of the congregation light other candles from it. It is lit again during all the services until Ascension Day, the fortieth day after Easter when Christians believe Jesus was taken up into heaven.

✝ OBEYING GOD

CHRISTIANS BELIEVE that they live their whole lives in sight of God. Every action, thought and sin is visible to him.

Confession and penance

All Christians pray for the forgiveness of their sins, but Roman Catholic and Orthodox Christians also tell their sins to their priest. This is called confession and may happen in a small private cubicle in the church. The priest gives a penance, or punishment, for the sins confessed, such as saying certain prayers. Penance is a sacrament in the Roman Catholic Church and is a sign that God has forgiven the person's sins.

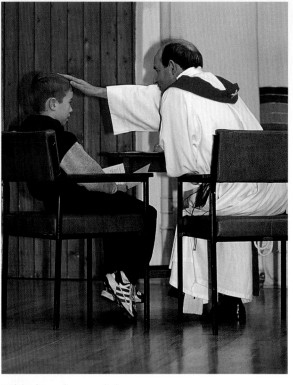

This boy is receiving a blessing from his priest after he has confessed his sins.

'Love the Lord your God with all your heart, with all your soul, and with all your mind.'

Matthew 22. 37

This Romanian girl is joining in a festival to honour the Virgin Mary.

Nuns dedicate their whole lives to God. These nuns are praying in a quiet place.

God's Commandments

In their lives, Christians try to keep God's rules, or commandments. In the Old Testament God gave his people a set of sacred rules called the Ten Commandments. These tell people to love only the one God, to keep the seventh day of the week holy, and to honour their parents. They forbid theft, murder, adultery, lying, envy and greed.

Jesus told his followers to keep the Ten Commandments. When asked by a Jewish scholar which was the greatest commandment, he answered: 'Love the Lord your God with all your heart, with all your soul and with all your mind.'

Monks and nuns

Most Christians think of God not just on Sundays but on every day of the week. Some especially devout Christians go even further. They give their whole lives to the worship of God and become monks or nuns. They take a vow of poverty and do not marry or take a job outside their monastery or convent. Today, many nuns and monks have a more modern lifestyle and work as teachers, healthcare workers or spiritual advisers.

✝ A CHRISTIAN LIFE

A CHRISTIAN LIFE is marked by several ceremonies in church: baptism, confirmation, marriage and, at death, a funeral.

Confirmation

Confirmation is a ceremony which confirms (or proves) that the Holy Spirit has come into a person and filled them with God's love. It used to be performed at the same time as baptism and in the Orthodox Church it still is, so that Orthodox Christians are confirmed when they are babies. But in other churches baptism and confirmation are now quite separate ceremonies.

This woman is being baptized as an adult.

Roman Catholic children are usually confirmed after their seventh birthday during Mass (a service celebrating the Eucharist). First they repeat their baptismal vows. Then the bishop extends his hands over them and prays that they may receive the Holy Spirit. He draws the sign of the cross on their forehead with chrism, a sacred fragrant oil. A similar service occurs in Protestant churches, although Protestants often do not get confirmed until they are teenagers, or even later. It is a solemn but joyous ceremony which celebrates someone becoming a full adult member of their church.

A priest uses holy water from a font to baptize a baby.

Marriage

Christians celebrate marriage as a blessing from God. The Bible says that the love between a husband and wife is sacred, like the love between Christians and God, and it instructs husbands and wives to support each other for the rest of their lives. The ceremony usually takes place in a church, in the sight of other Christians and, Christians believe, in the sight of God. In the ceremony the bride and groom promise to

love, protect and remain faithful to each other, while the priest prays that God will bless their marriage with happiness and children.

A Christian bride and groom are married by a priest in a church.

Death

A funeral is the final ceremony of a Christian's life. Christians believe that death is the moment of judgement when a person's soul will begin the journey either to be united with God for ever, or to be separated from him for ever. By Christ's sacrifice on the cross Christians know that their souls will be saved if they have believed in him and have asked for forgiveness for their sins. Death is therefore a time of sadness and joy. Christians are sad to lose someone they have loved on earth, but they rejoice to know that the person's soul is united with God in heaven.

Many Christians are buried in old, peaceful cemeteries like this one.

IMPORTANT DATES

c. 4BCE   Jesus is born in the land of Israel.

c. 28CE   Jesus is baptized in the River Jordan.

c. 30   Jesus is crucified. He rises from the dead three days later.

45–64   The apostle Paul preaches about Jesus in Cyprus, Turkey and Greece. Small Christian communities in these countries grow.

60–100   The four gospels are written. They become the first four books of the New Testament.

250–310   The Romans kill many Christians and destroy many churches.

313   The Roman Emperor Constantine promises Christians they can worship freely. Many people in the Roman Empire become Christians and the city of Rome becomes the centre of Christianity in western Europe.

381   Nicene Creed is written. It is still used in churches all over the world today.

386   Jerome, an Italian monk, begins to translate the Bible from Hebrew and Greek into Latin, the language of the Romans.

c. 400   The first monasteries appear in western Europe.

596   Bishop Augustine is sent from Rome to teach the English about Christianity. He becomes the first Archbishop of Canterbury.

1054   After many disagreements, the Church of Rome splits from the Church of Constantinople. This leaves the Roman Church, led by the Pope, powerful in western Europe, and the Orthodox Church powerful in eastern Europe and Russia.

1492   Christopher Columbus lands in the West Indies and claims the islands for Spain. Soon Spain sends missionaries to convert the Indians to Christianity.

1517   Martin Luther, a German monk, protests against the power of the Pope and corruption in the Catholic Church. This is the beginning of the great Protestant Reformation in which many Christians in northern Europe break away from the Roman Catholic Church and the rule of the Pope. These Christians are called Protestants.

1526   William Tyndale translates the Bible from Latin into English so that ordinary English Christians can read it for themselves. He is later killed by church leaders in England who believed that he was taking power away from them.

1534   Henry VIII, the King of England, abolishes the Pope's authority in England, and establishes the Anglican Church.

1542–52   Francis Xavier, a Jesuit monk from Spain, leads missions to Asia to try to convert the populations of India, China and Japan to Christianity.

1560   Under the leadership of John Knox, Scotland becomes a Protestant country.

1620   The ship, the *Mayflower,* carries a group of Puritans to North America to set up a new colony. The Puritans are strict Protestants who are unable to worship freely in England.

1647   In England, George Fox begins to organize the Society of Friends, or 'Quakers'. Quakers do not believe in killing people, and believe that people of all religions should live peacefully together.

1738   John Wesley begins to preach a simpler, plainer form of Christianity in England and America. This is the start of Methodism and is part of the Evangelical Revival, in which preachers reach out to poor and uneducated people with news of Christ's love for them.

c. 1800   Missionaries begin to travel all over the world to convert Indians, Africans, Chinese and other peoples to Christianity. The Bible is translated into many non-European languages.

1961   The World Council of Churches meets at New Delhi in India, bringing together Protestant and Orthodox churches from all over the world to celebrate their common faith in Jesus Christ.

1962–5   The Roman Catholic Church allows its services to be held in local languages rather than Latin which is now unknown to most of its congregations.

GLOSSARY

Apostle A messenger. One of Jesus's original followers or St Paul who, after Jesus's death, set out to spread the news of Jesus's coming to earth.

Ascension Jesus Christ's rising up into heaven forty days after he had returned to life after being killed on the cross.

Bishop A leader of all the churches in one area. A bishop is trained and given the authority to create priests and to perform confirmation.

Census A counting of all the people who live in a certain area.

Christ From Christos, the Greek word for Messiah. Because Jesus's early followers believed him to be the Messiah or King of the Jews, Jesus came to be called Christ and his followers Christians. See also: Messiah.

Congregation A group of people who worship at one church. To congregate is to gather together.

Covenant A solemn, firm agreement; a contract or a promise.

Crucifixion A way of killing someone by nailing them to a cross and leaving them without food or water.

Cubicle A tiny room. The cubicles used for confession in churches are about the size of a telephone box.

Denomination A grouping of Christians who all accept the same rules and believe in the same things. Baptists are one denomination; Anglicans and Lutherans are other denominations.

Disciple A follower; a person who accepts the teachings of a leader and passes on the teachings to other people. Jesus had twelve disciples.

Divine Coming from or belonging to God. Divine worship is worship which is devoted to God and which follows his rules on how to worship him.

Eternal Lasting forever.

Eucharist The sacrament of the Lord's Supper. It is also called the Mass or Holy Communion.

Gospel From the old English word *godspel* meaning 'Good News'. The first four books of the New Testament which tell of the life, death and resurrection of Jesus Christ are called the Gospels.

Hallowed Sacred; holy.

Martyr A Christian who is killed for being a Christian.

Messiah The saviour the Jewish books of the Old Testament promised would come to earth and restore the Jewish kingdom. Jesus's first followers believed Jesus to be the Messiah or the King of the Jews.

Nativity Birth. A nativity scene is a picture or model of the scene of Jesus's birth in the stable at Bethlehem.

Patriarchs The leading bishops of early Christianity, and the leading bishops of Orthodox Christianity today. The word patriarch simply means father.

Persecute To harass, bother or torture someone because of their religion, race or political beliefs.

Pope The leader of the Roman Catholic Church.

Prostitute A woman who earns money by having sex with men who pay her for it.

Repent To be sorry for; to regret. Someone who repents their sins is sorry for the wrong they have done and asks God to forgive them.

Resurrection Jesus's return to life after he had been crucified.

Rite A fixed set of rules for a ceremony such as baptism or marriage.

Salvation Being saved; achieving eternal life in heaven.

Saviour Someone who brings salvation, who can save a person from danger and evil. To Christians, Jesus Christ is their Saviour.

Scriptures The sacred writings of a religion.

Sin An act or thought which is wrong and which disobeys God's rules.

Soul The spirit of a person which exists separately from the body. Christians believe that after death the soul of a person goes to heaven or to hell.

Symbol An object or a picture which stands for something else without having to use exact words to explain it. For Christians, the cross is a symbol of Jesus Christ's sacrifice.

Virgin A person who has never had sex.

INDEX